See

BawB's Raven Feathers

Reflections on the simple things in life

VOLUME III

Robert Chomany

CALGARY, ALBERTA

ISBN 978-0-9918821-1-3 (v. 3 : bound)

Illustration: Jessee Wise
Book Design: Fiona Raven Book Design
Chief Editor: Rachel Small, Faultless Finish Editing
Proofreader: Carrie Mumford

Published by
Robert Chomany
Calgary, Alberta, Canada
bchomany@telusplanet.net

Printed in Canada by Friesens

www.bawbsravenfeathers.net

This series of books is dedicated to my mom—without her love, patience and guidance I would not be the man I am today. She taught me to appreciate compassion, to stand alone, to be proud of who I am and gave me strength to pursue my dreams.

I believe in who I am, I believe in what I know,
I believe my greatest gift of all is the smile that I can show.
I believe in who you are, I believe in what you do,
I believe there's no one else who is as good at being you.

Strength

Strength isn't always a measure of physical power, of how much weight one can lift in the gym. Strength is also measured by the soul. Your feelings, emotions, desires—how much can they endure? The strength of your will, how much you truly want something, often determines your level of personal growth. I have often heard the term "strong willed" and have wondered if there is a difference between strong willed and stubborn, and if so, can we be one without the other?

I have found in my travels that the strongest of men can also be the most compassionate; I have learned that strength comes from the soul, not from a bicep. Strength is a word that encompasses who we are as individuals—the particular strengths of our minds and bodies allow us to excel at some things and fail to grasp others. Some people find strength in their heritages, while others are not sure where they are from but are just as happy being who they are.

Women have inherited the strength of warriors, chieftains, doctors, politicians, and these days even hunter-gatherers. They show great strength as individuals and as contributors to society. And yet, the strength of a woman is often seen in the softness of her touch as she wipes the tears from a child's cheek, or in her ability to show great patience in the fast-paced corporate environment.

We all have our strengths, men and women, young and old, and we all share these strengths to become one society. When we are alone, we must call on our individual strengths to get us through times of challenge. We need strength to be who we are, to stand proud, and to be connected individuals in a busy world.

Step up my friends, take life as it comes,
be ready for any and all.
Believe in yourself and the strength in your soul—
stand up, be proud, be tall.

Strength is felt from deep inside,
it's nurtured in your soul,
for all those times you need the will
to help you achieve a goal.

Like the sun that shines above,
you have a light that's true.
You need to find your strength within
and trust in being you.

The path that you follow is not always easy,
you may often doubt your worth,
believe in you and find your strength
to walk on a path of soft earth.

Sometimes things will happen
and there's nothing you can do,
except to find your inner strength
and continue being you.

Never underestimate your will to succeed
and the strength you have inside.
It comes from your soul when you dig deep,
it's there beside your pride.

Don't fall prey to society's needs,
find a path where you belong.
Avoid the pressures of others' stress
and keep your spirit strong.
If you can't see the horizon each day,
then your head is not held high—
you should be seeing the morning sun
with a smile towards the sky.

No one can ever take from you
the feelings you keep within:
your heart and your soul, your inner strength,
are the reasons for your grin.

We have the strength inside of us
that will shine for all to see,
if only we can make the choice
to set our feelings free.

When you reach down deep to find some strength
and are left just feeling weak,
now is the time to believe in you
and shine that light you seek.
Nothing is ever as bad as it seems
if you can think in a positive way,
so live in the moment to deal with the worst;
tomorrow's a brand new day.

We wake each day repeatedly
never knowing what fate's in store;
we never know what's around that bend
or behind that unseen door.
Look to your strength and fortitude within
to help you every day,
to take on life with energy and smiles,
whatever comes your way.

Fear not the unknown and believe in your strengths;
they will cover short ambles as well as great lengths.

Will any words convince you
of how wonderful you are?
Is there any way to show you
that you are the brightest star?
Be strong today and quell the doubt
that clouds your honest view,
of how amazing you really are
at being beautiful you.

Belief

Do you believe? What do you believe? Do you believe in yourself? Have you ever been truly confident in who you are and what you can do? Maybe it's time to ask yourself if you are happy being you, and if the answer is no, then I believe it's time to make some changes.

Not long ago, you believed in Santa and the Easter Bunny. Do you remember when you stopped believing and why? The essence of these magical beings provided the energy we needed as kids to have fun, so if we as adults continued to believe in magical things, might we again be susceptible to having fun? Can you believe in the magic of yourself? If simply believing in something can enhance your life and make it more fun, then by all means, believe in you.

I think—no—I believe that if we put even a little energy into believing in ourselves a little more often, we would see a lot more smiles out there in the world. I also believe that if you choose to believe in yourself, then you will have the energy it takes to meet the challenges you face. And if you believe that the effort you put into something was your best, then even a failure or a rejection becomes a positive experience, a stepping stone towards the next attempt, and a lesson learned.

We all have our own minds, and we all form our own opinions, but as we grow, we can forget that sometimes believing in something is different from having an opinion. We can believe in whatever we choose and keep it to ourselves, but having an opinion involves sharing that belief with others. For example, I believe in my spirit guides, I believe my smile can be shared in the wind, and I believe in the strength of simply believing. These beliefs I tend keep to myself unless people ask, but I also have opinions on things that I openly share with all who will listen.

Believe in yourself to accomplish daily tasks, believe in yourself to jump hurdles and build confidence, and most importantly, believe in yourself because you will always be the best at being you.

Success is there within your view–

all you need is to believe in you.

Now is not the time to wonder
if you think you really can;
now is the time to believe in yourself
and follow through with your plan.

Can't is a word invented by those
who choose not even to try.
Soaring is easy, just spread your wings
and believe that you can fly.

Live your life with no regrets
and make sure your efforts are true.
Believe in what your future holds
because it's held for you.

Stay true to yourself and all you perceive,

stay focused and balanced and above all—believe.

The world becomes less formidable
when you believe in being you.
There is no place you cannot go,
and nothing you can't do.

One little thought that catches your attention
is all it takes to plant a seed of invention.

In order for dreams to materialize
you have to let your mind go.
You need to see the shapes in the clouds
and believe in what they show.

Dance to the drums that beat from your heart
and find your own forte,
believe in you and all you do
and be happy with each new day.

Don't be afraid to share your feelings–
take your inner self outside,
and believe in those who believe in you
with arms that open wide.
Don't expect to be the you
that everyone requires,
instead be happy being the one
who has faith in what transpires.

Believe in yourself and the direction you choose,
even when you have nowhere to go,
life is energy, it's always moving,
so relax and go with the flow.

Energy

Energy is life; it is the essence of all things; it is a river always flowing, always moving; it is visible in a smile or invisible in a summer breeze; it is as powerful as lightning and as warm as the noonday sun. Energy is in us all as we sleep and while we are awake, and if we are not careful, it can be unharnessed as anger. Energy is hard to describe in words because it is all encompassing. We are energy.

In my travels, I have gathered energy and shared it, I have spoken of it and learned about it, I have seen it in auras and felt it in a crowd of people. I would describe it as the feeling you get when you stand on a bridge and look down at a raging river. Energy is a signature—it is different in each and every one of us. There are those out there who can read energy, such as psychics, seers, and shamans, those who can feel energy in others, and those who think that energy lives only in their toasters, which is just fine, because we all think differently.

Energy is, from a human standpoint, our life force. The energy in our hearts pumps the blood that is vital, the energy in our lungs helps us to breathe the air, and the energy in our souls creates who we are as individuals. It is seen in our smiles and our frowns, it is expressed in our laughter and our tears. Our energy is who we are every second we exist, and I believe our energy is timeless. I like to think that we have actually existed in those times when we believe we are experiencing déjà vu—another time in another space, sharing the same energy in the same way.

We all share our energy with the world. Think of turning a space heater on in a room—the heat energy is shared by all. So if we all have wonderful energy, and we all share it in the same space of this tiny little planet, shouldn't a smile cast on one side of the earth be felt on the other side?

Smile while you think about that.

Your energy is your essence,
it's the you that people see first,
so take the time to put on a smile
should your day turn for the worst.

Believe in what you do,
your energy will actuate.
Be happy being you,
your energy will animate.

There is a peace within us,
it always comes out at night,
it lives among the quiet shadows
of the silver moon's half light.
Let your energy flow among the stars,
and glide on silent wing,
then greet the dawn with passion,
and welcome what life brings.

Breathe the air, feel the wind, spread your arms out wide,
the energy of life surrounds us all—welcome it with pride.

So you realize you're not the same
as everyone else today;
a different thought, a new idea,
you stand out in some way.
Embrace the difference, live for the moment,
be proud of being you,
your energy will simply shine
as you excel in what you do.

Your essence dances with the gentle wind
and is carried far and wide,
and your energy is a part of the earth,
like the ocean's flowing tide.

See, hear, feel the world around you, each and every day,
so much to do, places to be, things you need to say.
So many smiles you need to share and life you need to live,
the world enjoys the you that you are and all you have to give.

Can you feel the energy of distant friends?
Do you know when they're thinking of you?
Have you felt your heart suddenly skip a beat
when you're quietly just being you?
Energy flows to a balanced soul
like water in a sparkling stream,
and friends don't need to be in your presence
to tell you how much you mean.

Take away from a friendly chat
not just the voice that you heard,
but the warmth you felt from the energy
of the calmly spoken word.

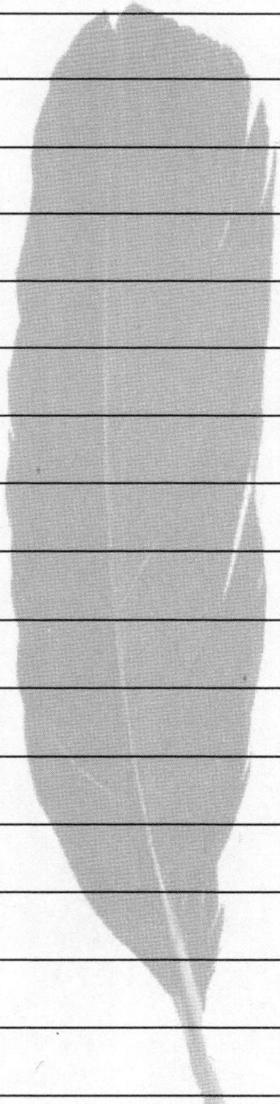

A lifetime ago or a minute from now—
our energy is timeless.
We walk our paths, we learn new things,
and our footprints mark our progress.

Like the echo returns the sound of your voice,
life will return the results of a choice.
If you're true to yourself and feel love in your soul,
then the world feels it too and will send it back whole.

The positive energy you let into your life
will eventually fill all the spaces,
and before you know it the people you meet
will soon have their own happy faces.
Energy flows from one to another,
it's a part of being real,
and when you share this positive energy,
it changes how you feel.

Positivity

I'm positive that I have mentioned this before, but just in case, I'll say it again—if you are positive in your belief of who you are, then all that happens to you will be positive. Basic life lesson 101: The Power of Positive Thinking. Positivity really does have a bearing on your adventures. For example, if you are positive that you will benefit by trying something new, then the venture will be a success, but if you are positive that you will fail and don't even try, then you immediately fail.

Everywhere you look you will see the positive if you choose to recognize it. I suppose if I were to get into the philosophy of positivity, I would mention that some folks believe we need rose-colored glasses to see the best in things, but I'm not going to go there because I believe we don't need glasses of any color to see what is right in front of us—what we need is the right attitude and some basic down-to-earth well being. I am positive that once happiness becomes a daily practice, well, things will just naturally start to look brighter.

Imagine what we could do with our energy if we chose to always make it positive. Imagine how this would affect every person you met and how in turn, that person's energy would spread positively. It really doesn't take much. In fact, I bet you would have to work harder to remain negative for any length of time, as there is just so much to smile about when you really put your mind to it. Yes, I know that there are skeptics who could point out all the evils and negativity in the world, but if even for a split second they think about something positive while reading this, then a spark will be ignited.

If you just can't think of something positive to think about right now, how about you share these words with others. And while you are sharing, you can smile. I am positive it will make a difference.

Positive energy is life's powerful force,

it keeps spirits high and presents a new course.

The power of thought is a wonderful tool–
it can take you far away.
With it you can create a space
where you feel you want to stay.
The power of positive thinking
is truly nothing short of real.
It's the only thing that you control
that shapes the way you feel.

Just by thinking positive thoughts
you can turn your world around.
You can shift dreams into ideas
that are exceptional and profound.

Do you ever feel that you can't keep up,
that life just flows on by?
Do you stand knee-deep in things to do
and wish that you could fly?
Cheer up my friends, you're on your way
to fixing this bit of plight;
just put on a smile and change your perspective,
then let yourself take flight.

As you stand there staring at the mountain ahead
and it feels like you're losing hope,
know your success is a thought away—
as the climb gets steeper,
just think like a goat.

With each new day comes a new adventure,
so accept things with an open mind.
If you can focus on positive energy
then your glass will be full, you'll find.

Strip away your negative side,
the one that casts all doubt,
and replace it with your positive side,
which you should never live without.

It doesn't matter how nice you are,
or if you love what's on your plate—
the world will have its negative souls,
and haters are going to hate.
Don't let these people get to you;
they are seeking a reaction.
Go on with your day in a positive way
and don't give them the satisfaction.

Never underestimate just what a smile can do:
it helps repel the negative and attracts good things to you.

The stress you carry can take physical shape,
like the stones along the shore,
so clear your mind of all the worry
and open every door.
Calm the waters that are your thoughts,
don't ever hold on to doubt,
just keep thinking positive things
and drive the negative out.

Share positive thoughts with the world that you meet,

and your path will be softer beneath your feet.

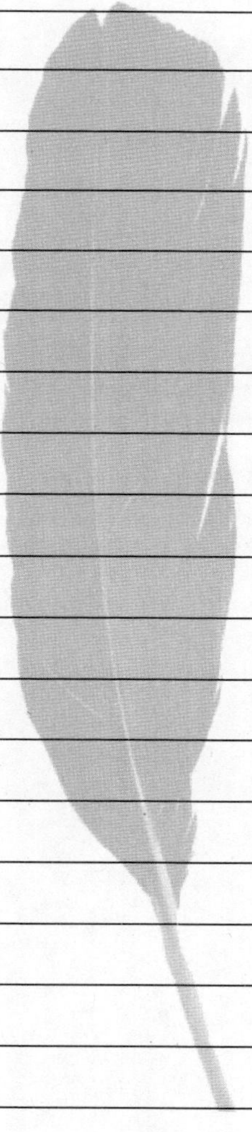

Like the water that brings life to us,
our energy flows in kind,
it can carry with it our positive,
and leave negative behind.
There is no time to dwell on things
that have no need or bearing,
you're better off to forge ahead
with a smile that's fit for sharing.

Balance

Balance, loosely defined, means trying to manage two unequal things. Balance is integral for a peaceful existence. The idea of balance has been around for centuries: Edison balanced the proper current with just the right element to improve the lightbulb, Da Vinci balanced his genius with his curiosity and poured the result into his art, and Plato balanced his wisdom with learning. Today, however, we live in a world where balance is challenged by the one-sided force of technology.

Our society is based largely on computers and other tools that steer us away from ourselves and nature. Perhaps this belief is extreme, but I have been watching the little things disappear in my short lifetime, like walks in the park on a sun-filled day. I am a big fan of change and the new, but balanced with tradition and the old.

Balance is always found in nature. It surrounds us daily, in the sun in harmony with the rain, in the wind that carries our energy and helps us share our inner light. We need spiritual harmony, a calm place, a haven to rest and gather strength. With balance, we can recognize our inner selves, our beings. We can choose to be happy and balance our happiness with the stressful ways of the world. We can't solve all the problems, but we can feel empathy for those who have them. We can choose to eat right when we can and balance the good food with a treat every now and then—everything in moderation. Too much of any one thing, like technology, will throw our lives out of whack and send out ripples of uncertainty or doubt.

It is not hard to realize balance. We need to welcome success as well as the lessons learned from failure; we need to compliment others by recognizing what they do and who they are while taking pride in everything we have contributed to help others succeed. With the aid of technology, we can communicate our successes, share smiles, and share our lives while complimenting all that others do in their adventures. But we should do this offline as well. If we take the time to enjoy our lives in many different ways, we can find balance.

Balance is more than just not tipping over,
it's also the center of living.
It softens extremes and helps you to choose–
it's the place between taking and giving.
You can find it inside, without really looking,
it helps you to care about life.
Balance is breathing and developing calm;
it will cut through your stress like a knife.

It's truly a gift, this thing we call living,
when we can balance receiving and giving.

If you are seeking simple balance
there is somewhere you can look:
it dwells within your kindest soul
and sounds like a laughing brook.

Balance is within us all, it keeps our world real,
it's in the wind around us, and changes how we feel.

Balance you'll find when you don't even try,

just lie back and relax with your eyes on the sky.

When you lose your balance for a minute or two
and your focus becomes a blur,
just settle your mind and remember to breathe,
'cause breathing is the cure.

Ask yourself a question
with each new day that comes—
am I remembering to balance
the serious and the fun?
There should be time enough for both
as you amble through your day,
so give your best at what you do,
but make it fun some way.

In order to add some balance to your day,
set yourself free when you can.
Push yourself back from your organized mess
and put walking into your plan.
The smile you show will let other folks know
that you are off in your mind having fun;
take your time, enjoy yourself,
your work will be there when you're done.

Take the time to focus today

on how much better you feel,

when you breathe in balance with every breath

and exhale the stress that is real.

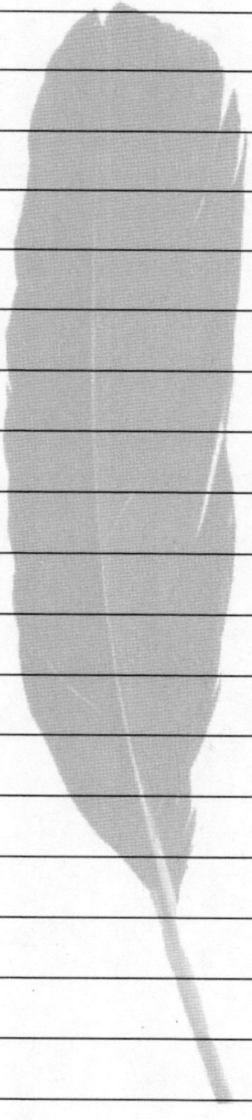

Whatever you do, have fun being you,
you don't need agendas to be.
Find a balance between being and doing
and the sun will be back, you'll see.

This is living, it happens each day,
over time it is called life;
make yours worthwhile when you have the chance:
choose balance over strife.

Renewal

When our energy is calm and balanced, we can renew our belief in ourselves. The earth must renew itself every day—sunshine, moonlight, tides, wind, rivers winding through valleys carved in rock. Everywhere we look, life is renewed in some way. And every day, we must renew our belief in who we are, in what we do. Every day we must be happy simply being. Renewal can be difficult in a hectic, rush-around, busy world. Sleep is not enough anymore. Our dreams are full of stresses and anxiety, and our lives are based on weekends alone. Mind, body, and spirit cannot be renewed in only two days.

We can renew ourselves with just a simple breath, a walk, a moment of calm to daydream, or better yet, through conversation with someone while wearing a smile. Enjoy just sitting, if only for a moment, then stretch and breathe. Always breathe, not just the air but also the energy around you. Renew your belief in others, compliment yourself and for goodness' sake compliment others, and find your strengths and work with them, appreciate them, share them. Help others to renew themselves—share your wisdom.

At night, give yourself a hug, hug the others in your life, and even hug your pets to renew their faith in you. Relax in your favorite chair or with someone else in his or her favorite chair and renew your love. Sleep because you want to, dream because you can. This period of stillness renews your strength and energy for the day that dawns anew.

Renew your curiosity and smile at the thought of trying something new. If you need to learn more about life or living in this great big world, or if you would like to fine-tune your imagination, then renew your library card. Life is about recycling your thoughts: old ideas, new dreams, old plans, new schemes. Have fun with what you have by enjoying it differently.

Look in the mirror in the morning and renew in yourself the belief that you are alive, you are important, and that others believe in you. Remind yourself that you can be happy being you because no one else could ever be the you that you have become.

With each new step you can welcome change
as being a simple gift,
a chance to create or postulate
and give yourself a lift.

Is it just too easy to accept what we have
and believe there's no other way?
Throw out the box you've been living in
and try something new today.
Color, sound, taste, or light,
see things through newfound eyes;
Then look around at what you have—
you're in for a surprise.

Sometimes you might feel that nothing is changing,
your life is always the same,
you see the things you've seen before,
and it starts to feel mundane.
But think for a moment when you stand by a river,
one that you've seen before—
it's the water that changes as it rushes past,
not the rocks along the shore.

Just when you think you've seen it all,
and the stories have been told,
try changing the way you look at life
and watch a new world unfold.

How can you say good morning today,
when in fact you're feeling blue?
How can you return a smile
when it's not coming naturally to you?
Take a deep breath and close your eyes,
for just one relaxing minute,
now bring to mind a happy thought
and smile at everything in it.
Release your breath and open your eyes,
then look at yourself in the mirror;
I'll bet you've found your smile again
and everything seems clearer.

Each new morning, when the sun hits your face,
is a chance for a brand new look:
a thousand new minutes to make some new memories
and share them in your book.

Our life is full of a million minutes,
each one should be enjoyed,
in order to make every moment important
a smile should be employed.
It’s not that easy to smile all the time,
some days it’s harder than others,
but those times will pass, they always do,
and soon your day will recover.

Another day, another dream,
another memory yet unseen.
We take each step, our prints in a row,
the more we see, the more we know.

Rid yourself of disparaging thoughts
that haven't gone away,
and fill the voids with happiness
that melts the gloom away.

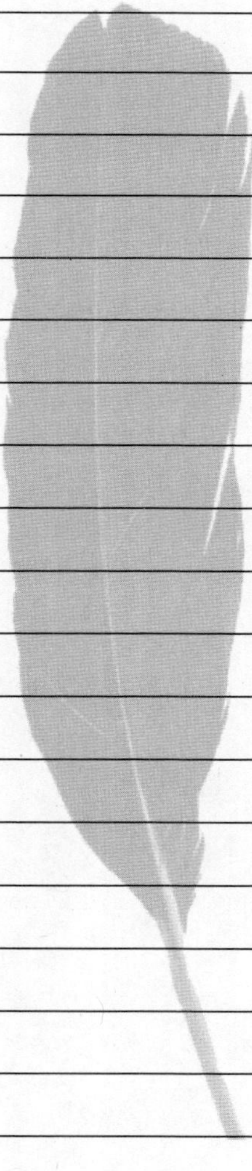

The earth lives by sharing the rain
with all that nature grows,
the beauty is seen when the skies then clear
and the abundant colors show.
The flowers bloom, the rivers flow,
life is always renewed,
so take each day with what it brings
and share a smile or two.

Onward today to brand new things,
listen to the wind and the new song it sings.
Take part in your life with an energized zest,
recognize challenges and give them your best.

Have I repeated too many times
the things that need to be said?
Have I written maybe once too often
the words that need to be read?
Can I express with too much effort
the fact that you are one of a kind?
The treasure that is within your heart
is something you need to find.
Believe in you and all that you do
and never give up on a quest;
shine the light that comes from your soul
and smile because you're the best.

Acknowledgements

I would like to thank the people in my life who have been there to help me along this new and uncharted path on which I walk.

Rachel Small - Editor, Faultless Finish Editing
Carrie Mumford - Proofreader
Jessee Wise - Illustrator
Fiona Raven - Designer

And to the souls in my life who have given me strength, support and inspiration, this adventure would not have happened without you all. Special thanks to all those who share my path, my life and my smiles.